OCCASIONAL
PAPER

Modernizing the
Federal Government

Paying for Performance

Silvia Montoya, John D. Graham

Sponsored by donors to the Pardee RAND Graduate School,
particularly Paul Volcker and Eugene and Maxine Rosenfeld

PARDEE RAND GRADUATE SCHOOL

The research contained in this report was made possible by the generosity of donors to the Pardee RAND Graduate School, particularly Paul Volcker and Eugene and Maxine Rosenfeld.

Library of Congress Cataloging-in-Publication Data

Montoya, Silvia.
    Modernizing the federal government : paying for performance / Silvia Montoya, John D. Graham.
      p. cm. — (Occasional paper)
    Includes bibliographical references.
    ISBN 978-0-8330-4323-8 (pbk. : alk. paper)
    1. United States—Officials and employees—Salaries, etc. 2. Personnel management—United States.
  3. Employee motivation—United States. I. Graham, John D. (John David), 1956– II. Title.

JK776.M74 2007
352.6'7—dc22

2007050579

The RAND Corporation is a nonprofit research organization providing objective analysis and effective solutions that address the challenges facing the public and private sectors around the world. RAND's publications do not necessarily reflect the opinions of its research clients and sponsors.

RAND® is a registered trademark.

Published 2007 by the RAND Corporation
1776 Main Street, P.O. Box 2138, Santa Monica, CA 90407-2138
1200 South Hayes Street, Arlington, VA 22202-5050
4570 Fifth Avenue, Suite 600, Pittsburgh, PA 15213-2665
RAND URL: http://www.rand.org/
To order RAND documents or to obtain additional information, contact
Distribution Services: Telephone: (310) 451-7002;
Fax: (310) 451-6915; Email: order@rand.org

Preface

This occasional paper examines the use of pay for performance in the federal government, one of the recommendations made in 2003 by the National Commission on the Public Service, also known as the Volcker Commission. It is based on a review of theoretical literature, demonstration projects, and current legislation regarding pay for performance. It should be of interest to presidential candidates and their staffs, cabinet secretaries, members of the civil service, members of Congress, the president, public administration scholars, and stakeholders seeking to influence federal employment and compensation policy.

Expert reviewers assisted the authors in generating the final version of the paper presented here. These reviewers were Jonathan Breul of the IBM Center for The Business of Government and Donald Arbuckle of the University of Texas at Dallas.

The research contained in this report was made possible by the generosity of donors to the Pardee RAND Graduate School, particularly Paul Volcker and Eugene and Maxine Rosenfeld. The authors gratefully acknowledge Diana Epstein, Elizabeth Brown, and Jane McClure for their review and comment on numerous early versions of the draft manuscript. The authors specially acknowledge previous research carried out by Teresa Taningco and the insights of Jennifer Hemmingway. All errors remain ours.

The Pardee RAND Graduate School is a recognized leader in doctoral education in policy analysis. Using a multidisciplinary approach, students and faculty examine a wide range of policy issues, including health, education, energy, public safety, and national and international security. Graduates pursue careers in universities, think tanks, public service, government, and the private sector. PRGS currently enrolls approximately 90 students, drawn from more than 20 countries around the world.

Contents

Figure

Tables

Summary

Pay for performance is a promising concept aimed at fostering productivity in the workplace. The anticipated impact comes from helping departments and agencies clarify their missions and goals, attract and retain quality employees, reward performance, and respond rapidly to changes in agency missions and priorities. Both theoretical and empirical evidence, much from the private sector, have shown that pay for performance faces a number of challenges: the cost of monitoring employee performance, the design of a useful appraisal system, the difficulty of linking appraisal systems to pay, and the unintended consequences of pay based on partial metrics of output. Transferring this concept from the private to the public sector is not easy because performance is often difficult to measure and civil servants may be less motivated by pay than private-sector employees.

Over the last three decades, the U.S. federal government pay structure has not been working in the desired way, despite the introduction of a merit-based pay component. Key problems include the difficulties associated with changing the seniority-based civil servant culture; the leniency bias in agencies' appraisal systems; the lack of rewards and consequences for outstanding and substandard performance, respectively; and the dearth of tools to address poor performance effectively. Valuable knowledge has been gained from demonstration projects in the U.S. Department of Defense, and more experience is accumulating with the implementation of alternative human resources systems in an increasing number of departments and agencies.

Proposals to change the General Schedule salary structure range from minor changes in the implementation of the General Schedule system (e.g., more training of managers) and more substantial modifications of compensation to more performance-based pay schemes. More recently, opposition to pay for performance has been growing and, thus, its future in the federal government is jeopardized. In our view, Congress should not prohibit or scale back pay for performance until the current experience is carefully evaluated. Moreover, the next administration should move to establish a pay system that will penalize those whose job performance is poor and reward those whose performance is outstanding; facilitate dialogue with employees and unions; and extend and evaluate pilot tests of new human resources systems.

Abbreviations

AFGE	American Federation of Government Employees
CCS	Contribution-Based Compensation System
CSRA	Civil Service Reform Act
DHS	Department of Homeland Security
DoD	Department of Defense
FAA	Federal Aviation Administration
FDIC	Federal Deposit Insurance Corporation
FY	fiscal year
GAO	Government Accountability Office
GPI	general price index
GPRA	Government Performance Results Act of 1993
GS	General Schedule
HR	human resources
IRS	Internal Revenue Service
MSPB	Merit System Protection Board
NA	not applicable
NIST	National Institute of Standards and Technology
NSPS	National Security Personnel System
OECD	Organisation for Economic Co-operation and Development
OMB	Office of Management and Budget

OPM	Office of Personnel Management
PART	Program Assessment Rating Tool
PASS	Performance Accountability and Standards System
PMRS	Performance Management and Recognition System
PFP	pay for performance
QSI	quality step increase
S.	Senate bill
SEA	Senior Executives Association
SES	Senior Executive Service
TSA	Transportation Security Administration
U.S.C.	United States Code
WGI	within-grade increase

PART ONE

Introduction

Improving productivity in government has been emphasized by the U.S. Congress since 1978, when the Civil Service Reform Act (CSRA) introduced a merit-based component to the salary of civil servants. The Government Performance Results Act of 1993 (GPRA) and the Program Assessment Rating Tool (PART) developed by the Office of Management and Budget (OMB) provided managers with tools to improve project management and deepened the pressure to ensure accountability for performance in the federal government. Alternative human resources (HR) systems have been authorized in the Department of Defense (DoD), the Department of Homeland Security (DHS), the Transportation Security Administration (TSA), the Central Intelligence Agency, the Internal Revenue Service (IRS), the National Institute of Standards and Technology (NIST), the Government Accountability Office (GAO),[1] the Federal Deposit Insurance Corporation (FDIC), and the Federal Aviation Administration (FAA), among other agencies. Performance-based pay is becoming a more prevalent feature of compensation systems, and by 2006 about 90,000 federal employees were in some form of performance-based system (Walsh, 2006).

The Bush administration aimed to transition the entire federal government into a performance-based system by 2010, allowing agencies to replace the seniority-based General Schedule (GS) salary system with more flexible pay systems. Performance-based pay is considered a promising tool to help departments and agencies clarify their missions and goals, attract and retain quality employees, reward performance, and respond rapidly to changes in agency missions and priorities.

This occasional paper explores the conceptual framework behind the pay-for-performance (PFP) scheme as well as the real-world experience with its implementation in the U.S. federal government. Our analysis illuminates whether the current structure of the GS provides the tools to properly distinguish substandard from excellent workers and reward them accordingly. As part of the study, we will also describe the recent reforms proposed by Senators Daniel Akaka (D-Hawaii) and George Voinovich (R-Ohio) in the 110th Congress and the burgeoning opposition to PFP that has developed in the new Congress.

---

[1] GAO was established as the General Accounting Office by the Budget and Accounting Act of 1921. Its name was changed to the Government Accountability Office in 2004. Both names are used within this document to accurately reflect when the GAO publications or findings were published.

PART TWO

Pay for Performance: Social Science Perspective

PFP began in the private sector and was introduced decades ago in the public sector as part of a movement to improve public-sector productivity, thereby producing better results from limited public funds. The underlying assumption is that a clear definition of goals, coupled with rewards for achieving these goals, will help motivate employees and enhance public-sector accountability. Edward Lazear, Professor of Human Resources Management and Economics at Stanford University and currently chairman of the Council of Economic Advisers in the Bush administration, has added to the list of its potential benefits the effect of PFP on employee selection, as incentive pay may attract better-performing job candidates (Lazear, 1996). The precise impact of incentive pay may vary with the nature of the job, the career path, and other key drivers of employment decisions.

Recent social science research on incentive systems stems from a number of perspectives: agency, expectancy, and goal-setting theory. Direct supervision is problematic or expensive in certain work environments and, therefore, a worker's effort is hard to monitor. New approaches stress the importance of incentives in order to motivate employees. Thus, motivation is a primary intervening variable between the incentive system and employee effort.

Agency theory stresses the role of performance incentives as a means of discouraging employees from "shirking" when management finds it costly to monitor their effort closely. It assumes that employees have some control over the effort they put into their work, that management finds it difficult to monitor effort, and that agents seek to maximize their individual utility. Under these conditions, if management were to offer a fixed time-rate of pay, theory predicts that employees will exert only the minimum effort they can get away with (Lazear, 1995).

Management can respond by linking pay to a variable that is correlated with output or performance. Thus, an important component of the theory is that employees will respond to performance pay because it gives them an incentive. This is also true of many employees who shirk. According to the theory, they shirk not out of laziness, but because the structure of incentives does not foster effort. Alternatively, the employer might invest more in performance measurement to improve the correlation between effort and measures of output. In a strict sense, a cost-minimizing employer would evaluate the costs of monitoring versus the costs of paying a higher wage to employees to encourage effort. He would decide in favor of the more cost-effective alternative.

Collective agreements or equity considerations may constrain how large pay differentials can be. Theory suggests that organizations with risk-averse employees (often those in the public sector) will find it more advantageous to improve appraisal systems rather than increase financial rewards. Hence, the quality of performance monitoring depends on goal setting and valid appraisal.

Finally, agency theory postulates that rewarding individual performance will encourage employees to boost their own performance and, if necessary, reduce cooperation with their colleagues. This trade-off suggests that we should consider both incentive and divisiveness effects of individual PFP schemes.

Expectancy theory places a strong emphasis on the motivational effects of pay incentives. In a simplified version, it identifies a potentially virtuous circle (Vroom, 1964; Porter and Lawler, 1968). Employees will respond to an incentive or reward if they value it (validity), if they believe good performance will be instrumental in bringing the desired reward (instrumentality), and if they expect their efforts will achieve the desired performance (expectancy).

The circle of "validity-instrumentality-expectancy" can be broken at a number of points: when employees feel they lack the ability to increase their effort, when they feel their effort will make little difference to their performance, and when they believe that management lacks either the competence or the good faith (or both) to evaluate and reward fairly. All of the above situations may cause employees to view PFP schemes as unfair and divisive. This perspective shares two critical assumptions with agency theory: that employees can choose between different levels of effort and that motivation is a prime determinant of the level of effort selected by the employee.

Goal-setting theory stresses the motivating power of defining appropriate work goals and engaging employee commitment to those goals. The potential inducement of rewards is considered to be secondary. Of particular relevance in the current context is the emphasis on dialogue between line managers and employees, wherein they exchange information about realistic goals and come to agreement so that employees adopt goals as their own.

David Marsden, Professor of Labour Markets at the Centre for Economic Performance of the London School of Economics, argues that the introduction of PFP achieves a renegotiation of the "effort-for-pay" bargain (Marsden, 2004). Renegotiating the effort bargain is different from discouraging shirking. Unlike the latter, there is no reference to moral hazard, that is, no reference to the lack of workers' effort due to the absence of monitoring instruments. Because it concerns the move from one agreed exchange of effort for pay to a new, often higher one, it raises productivity without criticizing the prior levels of effort.

One can imagine renegotiation of effort as a game that would gradually bring management and employees into a cooperative equilibrium. Neither side seeks to use every unanticipated change as a pretext for renewed negotiations. If each party knows that micro-bargaining will harm the other, they can cooperate and share information. Recurrent renegotiation of the ground rules can undermine this equilibrium and lend itself to opportunistic behaviors.

The transition between two radically different pay systems in the public sector (e.g., moving from seniority-based to performance-based rewards) involves a major renegotiation of effort and might demand some control of the process to avoid a slide into uncontrolled micro-bargaining. Employees, on the one hand, might be suspicious that effort demands will be heightened and that management will manipulate appraisal scores with the goal of either saving money or rewarding their favorite employees (Marsden and French, 1998). Managers, on the other hand, face risks associated with not being able to measure performance effectively should they seek to avoid conflict or to prevent certain employees from leaving. The generalized upward drift in performance ratings is considered to be a sign of the difficulties managers have in keeping appraisal systems under control.

Some authors argue that PFP serves more as a tool for improving management processes rather than motivating staff (Organisation for Economic Co-operation and Development [OECD], 2005). Three points have been raised about management changes:

1. Employees are supposed to take a training course as a requirement to receive a bonus.
2. PFP can be used as a way to introduce new methods of work, reorganize work in order to introduce more flexibility, and provide a more responsive service to the public.
3. PFP may therefore encourage innovation and risk taking in organizations. In the delivery of services (health, education, tax collection, social security), where teamwork needs to be responsive to the needs of citizens, this case for PFP may be especially applicable.

Furthermore, PFP facilitates wide organizational changes by linking bonuses to new objectives at the individual and departmental levels. OECD (2005) provides evidence that might support the former hypothesis: PFP has been associated with deep changes in some paradigms in the public sector (e.g., how agencies are organized and whether jobs are defined in terms of performance expectations rather than in terms of formal tasks or responsibilities).

There is some evidence from the UK that, contrary to presumptions, the introduction of PFP schemes discourages employees. Marsden and French (1998) show that only a small fraction of employees perceive that performance schemes induce work beyond job requirements or stimulate more initiative. Performance pay schemes were seen by staff to be divisive and to undermine cooperation among staff.

Despite the initial disappointment, a second study of the National Health Service (UK) confirmed that employees who experienced well-conducted appraisals by their managers were likely to find PFP schemes motivating, while those who experienced the opposite find PFP schemes demotivating and damaging to work relations. Thus, the experience with PFP in the UK has been mixed, with varying effects on individual performance. Nevertheless, the link between PFP and motivation needs further research in real-world settings—e.g., the impact of rewards on substandard performers and the impact on motivation when outstanding employees perceive the award as a form of entitlement.

Unfortunately, most of the research has been done on PFP design. Experience from both OECD and non-OECD countries suggests that adequate implementation is crucial for PFP effectiveness. Some of the issues raised include

*   the need for clear organizational objectives and manager training in operating the scheme
*   the importance of consultation with staff (1) to facilitate employee buy-in and (2) to ensure that employees' concerns get conveyed to managers
*   reliance—at least partially—on goal setting, rather than on standard criteria for the job in the definition of the scheme
*   the availability of funds for the new scheme (Risher, 2004)
*   the need for system transparency (OECD, 2005; Ketelaar, Manning, and Turkisch, 2007).

Consideration should be given to team performance pay systems since some evidence indicates that such approaches have had beneficial effects (in Finland, Germany, Korea, and the United Kingdom) (OECD, 2005).

In sum, the theoretical and applied literature on PFP provides indications that PFP is a promising concept. But the real-world application of the tool confronts pitfalls that need to be carefully studied to ensure effectiveness without adverse side effects. In some settings, PFP may need to be combined with other tools in order to be effective.

PART THREE

PFP: Different Forms

Conceptually, PFP refers to compensation that is directly tied to specific performance. As theoretically appealing as it is, paying for performance has a variety of forms and definitions (see Table 3.1). And it demands some level of budget control when it comes to implementation. Measures may be applicable at the individual or organizational/unit/team level. In some cases, the combination of individual and collective schemes is a solution to deal with the problems associated with each of them. Such a system rewards outstanding team effort and exceptional individuals within the team.

In PFP, what matters are the marginal increases in pay as opposed to average pay (see items 4 and 5 in Figure 3.1). Base pay is important for recruitment and retention, but the marginal increase in pay is what may motivate performance, since it allows workers to receive larger wage increases without having to wait for a promotion.

The effective use of PFP as a managerial tool assumes that managers are able to exert some control over their budget and can add some components to the pay received by their employees. When pay systems are very centralized and there is little room for changes, the success of PFP is unlikely. Decentralization of PFP and budgetary management reduces these problems but raises issues related to equity across agencies and departments. The challenge with decentralization is to devise accountability and control mechanisms that check for potential unfairness.

Incentives for performance may be provided through means other than explicit PFP. Promotion, career opportunities, and seniority-based systems are examples of incentive structures that are not explicitly based on performance measures. When there is a link between

Table 3.1
Alternative Forms of PFP

Form	Pros	Cons
Merit increments	Produce long-term incentive	Tend to become automatic
Bonuses	Offer more flexibility and are visibly related to performance	May only create short-term incentive
Large performance payments per individual	Create a positive and immediate impact on motivation	May have a negative impact on employees who do not receive the bonus
Small performance payments	Allow for the possibility of distributing across staff	May have a limited impact on motivation
Limited number of recipients (quotas)	Sustain a clear system for performance differentiation	Appear to have arbitrary limits

SOURCE: Based on OECD (2005).

Figure 3.1
Principal Components of Compensation with PFP

Basic pay

+ Allowances

+ Automatic increases

+ Group performance

+ Individual performance
_____

Total compensation

RAND *OP213-3.1*

performance and pay, the forms it can take are diverse, including the degree of formality required to justify the additional pay.

Individual performance payments have been widely used for a long time, but were traditionally used over and above the annual pay award and were largely concentrated in white-collar managerial occupations. Since the 1980s, PFP schemes have been modified to account for organizational objectives. In short, there is a range of different PFP schemes, which utilize a variety of individual and team-based criteria for making such rewards.

PART FOUR

The Appraisal System: A Source of Concern

PFP is difficult to implement in government agencies because it is extremely challenging to measure output or to track performance. The evaluation method used to decide whether or not to award wage increases can be subjective (based on a supervisor's opinion) or objective (associated with some observable output).

It is often argued that a subjective performance assessment can provide a more complete measure of performance by taking into account not only the output itself but also whether the action of the employee or unit that led to that output was appropriate under the circumstances (Prendergast, 1999). Furthermore, nonquantifiable aspects of jobs are extremely important, and a manager's subjective evaluation of those aspects can provide a more accurate appraisal than only quantifiable indicators. Subjective evaluation also has the advantage of eliminating the problem derived from restricting the measure of output to only one dimension (for example, the exclusive reliance on test scores in education).

OECD (1994) has described the public service pay systems prevalent in developed countries. Countries have chosen not only a variety of "output" indicators but also competencies and technical skills, interpersonal skills and teamwork, leadership and management skills, and other inputs. New Zealand, Australia, and Sweden rely exclusively on output to define objectives; Italy and Switzerland also add interpersonal and managerial skills to the schemes. Denmark, Finland, Austria, Ireland, Poland, Korea, France, and Germany combine output objectives with improvement in technical skills, while former socialist countries like the Czech and Slovak Republics rely more on values, discipline, and inputs. Canada, Portugal, Spain, and the United Kingdom use a combination of different criteria. Some countries, e.g., Canada and Denmark, also consider ethics and innovation, respectively (OECD, 2005; Ketelaar, Manning, and Turkisch, 2007).

Performance appraisal is commonly based on job objectives. The process of performance management is usually an annual cycle, in which the line manager identifies key objectives for the year with his or her employee(s), generally in line with organizational goals. After a period of time (the "appraisal period")—generally one year—the employee's performance is assessed by his or her manager.

The appraisal system is a crucial part of any subjective PFP scheme, and a variety of issues are being studied in the research literature. Not only have formats received attention, but researchers are also studying the existence of subconscious effects on ratings, the sources of ratings, and the effects of "rater/ratee" characteristics. However, studies on issues such as fairness, the actual uses of appraisals, and the real-world consequences of appraisals are limited and much research remains to be done for both the private and the public sector.

Part of the problem is that most of the PFP research has been done in experimental settings using cognitive perspectives. This branch of the psychology draws inferences about mental processes by observing human behavior. In terms of performance appraisal, research has concentrated on analyzing how expectations or knowledge about prior performance level affects the rating process.

Raters' knowledge of prior performance affects raters' information processing by anchoring current judgments. Additionally, it has been found that raters' expectations may introduce bias in rating. For instance, Mount and Thompson (1987) observed that appraisal results were more accurate when observed and expected behaviors were similar. Research also suggests that job and ratee knowledge have significant effects on the subconscious internal appraisal by the appraiser (i.e., a "halo" effect).

Discrepancies of ratings across raters have also attracted research effort. Some studies suggest that rating dispersion among raters regarding the same employee's performance is related to the weight raters assign to job-related inputs; raters give scores according to how the employee performs in the area salient to the rater.

Personal Characteristics

In terms of rater/ratee characteristics, research on gender effects has yielded conflicting results. For example, no sex (or race) effects were reported in field settings where job analysis was used to develop a task-based performance appraisal instrument. Conversely, students tend to give women professors higher ratings (Bretz, Milkovich, and Read, 1992). Benedict and Levine (1988) demonstrated that females were more lenient with poorly performing employees and delayed performance appraisals and feedback sessions more than males did. However, gender and race account for an extremely small amount of variance in ratings.

Rater Training

Research reviews (mostly for the private sector) have concluded that rater training has not been highly effective in increasing the accuracy of ratings. However, there is some contrary evidence suggesting that training can lead to more accurate ratings—particularly training that focuses on the rating process and on the use of specific rating tools (Milkovich and Wigdor, 1991).

OECD (2005) has found that practical training on evaluation combined with simplicity and transparency in evaluation systems has helped successful implementation of PFP. In the case of the U.S. federal government, officials at agencies that are successfully using PFP systems say that training has been crucial to keep the system fair (Walsh, 2006). For example, the FAA used printed media, interactive technology, and webcasts to educate both employees and supervisors on the new system. At FDIC, every manager and supervisor received training when the agency phased in its pay-for-performance system. The DoD has built a system of checks and balances into its review process: Each review will be examined by another set of eyes looking at or for "troubling trends" (Walsh, 2006).

OECD concludes, based on HR surveys, that the likelihood of positive results for appraisal systems depends principally on five factors:

1. simplicity of the design
2. definition of objectives and goals
3. assurance of correlation between appraisal and financial rewards
4. manager's training in operating the system
5. implementation by line managers (OECD, 2005).

In sum, although knowledge of the rating process has expanded in recent years, understanding of how PFP works in practice remains fragmented. Research is only beginning to address how the environment affects employee perceptions of appraisal, their reactions to appraisal outcomes, and how appraisal purpose influences these relationships.

PART FIVE

PFP in the Public Sector: Evidence

PFP originated in the private sector, where opposition to automatic salary increases is often considered as a "philosophical issue" (Risher, 2004). It works in the private sector as much through the recruiting mechanism for performance (Lazear, 1996) as it does through incentives for existing employees. However, evidence from private-sector establishments suggests that only 9.4 percent of full-time workers are paid on the basis of piece-rate (pay per unit of work) measures and only 14.2 percent are paid with bonuses (Asch, 2005).

The translation of PFP from the private sector to the public sector is not straightforward. For example, measurement of output or performance may be more difficult in the public sector, and the reliance on incentives through motivation does not necessarily work as it does in the private sector, where the feasibility of firing poorly performing employees helps to reinforce the scheme. Public servants do not typically have "at will" contracts. This makes the firing of poorly performing employees more difficult than in the private sector. The sidebar on page 14 (Teachers' Salaries: PFP or Pay for Seniority?) reveals some of the challenges in applying PFP to public school teachers.

Most OECD countries have a formal performance appraisal system for civil servants, often based on an individual assessment of performance. Such assessments rely largely on job objectives as defined in a general employee/management performance agreement, rather than on generalized criteria for a given job. Most countries have developed a different performance management system for senior managers.

Very few countries have developed systematic policies to address underperformance (OECD, 2005). Career civil service systems traditionally have procedures that generally address misconduct, not procedures designed to improve the performance of underperformers. Unfortunately, research is needed to determine whether poor performance is protected by the tightness of public employee firing regulations and the strength of public-sector unions.

Regarding how PFP has been introduced, experiences are diverse in OECD countries. Germany, Hungary, Italy, Spain, Switzerland, and the United States have enacted laws. Denmark, Finland, and Sweden have reached collective agreements. Canada, New Zealand, and the United Kingdom have found their own mechanisms (policy advice, bargaining parameter, and negotiations with the Cabinet Office and HM Treasury, respectively) to establish merit pay for civil servants (OECD, 2005).

Teachers' Salaries: PFP or Pay for Seniority?

PFP was introduced in the American educational system in the 1980s with the objective of improving student learning outcomes. It was thought that a merit-based system was going to produce better results than the single-salary schedule prevalent in the sector. However, the idea of rewarding teachers according to students' outcomes in standardized tests has been criticized with a variety of arguments about the unique features of teaching (e.g., motivation, team production, multitasking) and the risk that schools would focus only on preparing for the test while disregarding other activities (Podgursky and Springer, 2007).

An assessment of alternative U.S. K–12 payment systems concluded that payment for output is superior to payment for input (teacher certification, seniority, etc.) in terms of raising overall productivity (Lazear, 2000). Teacher certification and experience serve in the hiring stage as a proxy for productivity. But PFP will attract and retain individuals who are good at the task to which incentives are attached as long as they know that, given the same levels of certification and experience, they will earn more. Lazear (2000) finds evidence supporting the existence of sorting effects: In the absence of PFP incentives, highly capable teachers are more likely to leave the profession than less-capable teachers.

A recent evaluation of U.S. teachers' performance systems shows, based on a large number of incentive programs, that while no connection, positive or negative, has been found between student outcomes and teacher certification, the correlation between student outcomes and incentive programs was positive, especially in the private sector (Podgursky and Springer, 2007).

In a very recent development, Mayor Bloomberg's administration and the New York City teachers union announced an agreement on October 17, 2007, regarding a performance-pay plan that gives teachers bonuses largely on the basis of test scores of students at schools with high-poverty populations. New York's plan is a twist on the traditional concept of performance pay. Money will be given to schools that do a good job raising students' test scores but will not be distributed teacher by teacher (Gootman, 2007).

Part of the challenge of implementing PFP lies in the culture that emerged as a consequence of the tenure-based civil service pay system. For instance, in the United States, FDIC has taken four plans and more than five years to implement a merit-based system (Mendelsohn, 2007). It has been argued by some federal employees and representatives of the employees union that giving managers and supervisors so much power over an employee's fate will "breed favoritism, … lower morale and erode the spirit of teamwork on which public service is based" (Walsh, 2006).

A recent study of more than ten OECD countries indicates that the impact of PFP on motivation is indeterminate: While it appears to motivate a minority of staff, it seems that the majority do not see PFP as an incentive (Marsden, 2004). Burgess and Ratto (2003) found that lack of motivation is not a characteristic problem of UK civil servants. The apparent inefficacy of the PFP system has led to some extreme decisions to withdraw the system (e.g., for the police in New Zealand). In most cases when PFP is questioned, total elimination is not an option; instead, governments have switched from an individual PFP system to a team-based system (e.g., in areas such as education, where teamwork was considered crucial to success).

Moreover, the effectiveness of PFP in making the civil service more attractive to high-quality employees has also been questioned. PFP may have a limited recruitment effect in the public sector because of the small size and the contingent nature of the rewards. Factors such as job content and career development prospects may be the prime drivers of recruitment. Promotion also has limitations as a generalized incentive: Even when there is the potential for promotion, it may be slow when the amount of employment in public services is stable or declining. The aging of the workforce in the public sector has resulted in large numbers of employees staying at the same rate of pay or within narrow pay bands for years.

Criteria such as satisfying job content, promotion possibilities, or flexibility in work organization come far ahead of performance pay in motivating staff. The evidence points, therefore, to the need for a broad approach to better performance management as opposed to an exclusive focus on performance-related compensation.

Pay for Performance in the State Systems

Efforts to link individual performance to pay are widespread at the state government level. In the early 1990s, at least 24 states had already created PFP systems (Ingraham, 1993). The GAO, in a survey of states that had enacted PFP by the end of the 1980s, found an uneven coverage of the labor force: While Atlanta only covered the top managers in the state (400 at that time), Oregon included two departments and Arizona had 68 percent of civil servants covered by PFP schemes. Unionization helps explain the dispersion (U.S. General Accounting Office, 1990). It was also mentioned that the form of the rewards was diverse; PFP may encompass onetime bonuses added to base pay or a combination of both.

There were also similarities in the state systems regarding the rating system: Half of them were using a 5-point rating system and half a 3-point system. In most states, the performance rating was tied to the size of the award (U.S. General Accounting Office, 1990). The GAO found that the budget for PFP is a key issue in the introduction of PFP. In most cases, money was derived by "setting aside a small proportion of the total personnel budget or from savings within a specific department" (Ingraham, 1993, p. 193). As a result, there was general dissatisfaction with size of the performance awards.

Ingraham (1993) points out that the chances of PFP being introduced and extended in the states depends on the state's civil-service history and age. New York has a highly centralized and old system while others (e.g., Virginia) have reformed, decentralized state personnel processes. Ingraham (1993) suggests as a hypothesis that the states with the more chronic funding problems are more likely to introduce PFP, since it is seen as a tool for better budget management.

Some researchers have collected employee and manager perceptions of their PFP state system. Kellough and Selden (1997) report that around 60 percent of the managers that responded thought PFP was effective. Kellough and Nigro (2002), describing the finding for the GeorgiaGain Program, mention that 85 percent of the employees believed that managers had imposed quotas or limits on outstanding performance while only 50 percent of them agreed that their most recent performance rating accurately reflected their performances (p. 153).

Complaints were linked, in general, to human or technical errors or insufficient funds. Kellough and Nigro (2002) highlight that, when asked to rank the difficulties with PFP schemes, the most commonly experienced problems are the lack of adequate funding of the systems (related to both lack of sufficient funding and fixed PFP budgets) and the difficulties in developing and implementing good performance measures.

Local governments have also been active in the development and use of performance measurement processes. Melkers and Willoughby (2002) found that the application of performance measurement to decisionmaking was fairly widespread among local governments by 2000, but the extent to which it was used in budgeting and other decisionmaking varied dramatically between city and counties.

PART SIX

PFP in the U.S. Federal Government

The Pendleton Civil Service Reform Act of 1883 established the Civil Service Commission and is the first U.S. law related to civil service. The act, which applied only to federal jobs, placed most employees on the merit system. The act also made it unlawful to fire or to demote federal employees for political reasons. The law further forbade requiring employees to give political service or contributions. "One result was more expertise and less politics" (U.S. Office of Personnel Management, 2007).

The Classification Act of 1923 went one step further. The act divided work into five services (professional and scientific, subprofessional, clerical, custodial, and clerical-mechanical) and covered only headquarters positions. The 1923 act introduced the principle of "equal compensation for equal work irrespective of sex," which was a significant shift from past practice in both the public and private sectors. Later on, the Classification Act of 1949 introduced the General Schedule, or GS system, nationwide and consolidated the three first categories of the Classification Act of 1923 (professional and scientific, subprofessional, and clerical employees). Since then, the GS has become the core of the pay system.

In 1978, the CSRA refined the GS structure by (a) creating the Senior Executive Service (SES) (a separate employment and pay system covering employees formerly in GS grades 16, 17, and 18); (b) creating the Merit Pay System for managerial (nonbargaining unit) employees in GS grades 13, 14, and 15; and (c) giving potential room for pay systems to evolve by creating authority for demonstration projects to test HR system improvements for later government-wide application.

With the Performance Management and Recognition System (PMRS) and the Federal Employees Pay Comparability Act of 1990, the process for maintaining and adjusting the pay system was refined. Agencies were given a high degree of freedom to define and align individual and organizational performance. Several personnel systems were excepted from GS provisions, and alternative approaches to classification and pay began to be used.

In concert with the effort to encourage worker productivity, other tools were provided to departments to help them design their activities in relation to the overall agency mission. This is a crucial element in any successful performance management plan. GPRA requires agencies to engage in project management tasks such as setting goals, measuring results, and reporting their progress. As part of this effort, PART was developed by OMB to assess and improve program performance so that the federal government could achieve better results. A PART review looks at all factors that affect program performance including design; performance measurement, evaluations, and strategic planning; management; and results.

The GS has roots in the Classification Act of 1949 and is codified as part of Chapter 53 of Title 5 of the United States Code (5 U.S.C.), sections 5331–5338. The Wage Grade schedule includes most federal blue-collar workers. The Office of Personnel Management (OPM) administers the GS pay schedule on behalf of other federal agencies, although changes to the GS must normally be authorized by the president (via executive order) or by Congress (via legislation).

According to Damp (2002), "There are eight predominant pay systems. Approximately half of the workforce is under the General Schedule (GS) pay scale, twenty percent are paid under the Postal Service rates, and about ten percent are paid under the Prevailing Rate Schedule (WG) Wage Grade classification. The remaining pay systems are for the Executive Schedule, Foreign Service, Nonappropriated Fund Instrumentalities pay scales, and Veterans Health Administration." Some government agencies use alternative pay systems (e.g., the IRS, NIST, the GAO, FDIC, and the FAA). Alternative pay systems are also being implemented at the DHS and the DoD and in the SES, which has been under such a system since January 2004 (Walsh, 2006).

The GS defines grade levels by describing levels for skill and knowledge, responsibility, physical effort, and working conditions. Within the GS, each agency may develop one or more appraisal systems. The appraisal systems shall provide for periodic appraisals of job performance of employees and encourage employee participation in the establishment of performance standards. Furthermore, the results of performance appraisals shall be used as a basis for training, rewarding, reassigning, promoting, reducing in grade, retaining, and removing employees.

Under the CSRA, the OPM and the Merit System Protection Board (MSPB) were created to replace the U.S. Civil Service Commission. Aside from creating the SES and establishing the Federal Labor Relations Authority, the CSRA also established a system of performance-related pay for GS-12 to GS-15 federal employees. Moreover, the CSRA also set up experiments giving line managers more control over personnel decisions.

The GS Structure

In order to appreciate the controversy about PFP, it is helpful to understand how the majority of federal civil servants are paid under the GS pay structure. There is a schedule of annual rates of basic pay consisting of 15 grades, designated GS-1 through GS-15, with 10 pay steps per grade. In general, grades 1–7 are entry levels, grades 8–12 are mid levels, and the rest are senior levels.

The GS pay structure has two basic determinants: tenure and performance. For all employees in a regular position who have not yet reached the maximum rate of pay within their grade, federal law mandates a regular "within-grade increase" (WGI), or step increase, as long as the employee has demonstrated an acceptable level of performance (U.S.C. 5335). Each grade has a pay range of 30 percent, with each step increasing the previous level of base pay by an average of 3 percent; the percentage increase declines as the grade increases (e.g., an average of 1.7 percent between, say, GS-14 and -15).

Per 5 U.S.C., an employee in a permanent position within the scope of the GS who has not reached the maximum step in the grade will be automatically promoted within the grade by completing a certain number of weeks of work. The requirements vary depending on the grade: 52 weeks in pay rates 1, 2, and 3; 104 weeks in pay rates 4, 5, and 6; and 156 calendar weeks in pay rates 7, 8, and 9 (U.S.C. 5335). The "schedule" ensures that employees will progress from one step to the next if they accumulate enough years of tenure. Table 6.1 describes the form and size of performance-based pay within the GS.

Table 6.1
Form and Maximum Size of Individual PFP in the GS

Merit Increases	Bonuses
An employee who meets a high performance bar may be advanced to the next step (QSI).	An employee who delivers above-average performance may be granted a cash performance bonus (typically 1–2 percent of the salary).
An agency may advance an employee who meets a high performance bar to the next step of a grade (approximately a 3 percent increase).	Cash bonuses of up to 10 percent of base pay can also be paid to managers. In the case of unusually outstanding performance, the bonus could be up to 20 percent of base pay.

NOTE: Funding for both QSIs and bonuses is provided out of the regular budget for salaries and expenses.

The merit increases have two components: promotion through a quality step increase (QSI) and performance-based cash awards. The QSIs are faster than normal WGIs, and are used to reward employees who deliver superb performance. To be eligible for a QSI, employees must have received the highest rating available and have demonstrated sustained performance of high quality. QSIs may be received no more than once each 52 calendar-weeks. In unusual cases, a high-performing employee may be promoted to the next higher grade more quickly than the agency's normal time-in-grade guidelines, but in no case sooner than 12 months (U.S.C. 5336). Unlike lump-sum awards, QSIs represent a cost to the agency on an ongoing basis; QSIs increase retirement and Thrift Savings Plan expenses.

Performance bonuses are lump-sum cash awards based on performance ratings. Agencies can use the rating of record as the sole basis for granting them. Some departments and agencies also award onetime bonuses (cash or noncash) based on performance. For instance, in fiscal year (FY) 2006, 67 percent of federal executives received a bonus, with some agencies having an even larger share of their executives receiving this kind of award (Barr, 2007a).

Federal workers may also be appointed to positions with "career ladders" or "targeted positions" and other terms. Career ladder promotions are a series of developmental positions of increasing difficulty through which an employee may be promoted to higher grades without competition (U.S. General Accounting Office, 2004). Once one grade is completed, employees whose performance is acceptable will typically (but not automatically) be promoted by management to the next grade in the ladder, near the anniversary of the employee's appointment. This is typical for many professional positions designed for college graduates. For example, a recent college graduate with a bachelor's degree may take a GS position at the GS-5 or GS-7 level, depending on the job itself, the individual's academic achievement, prior experience, and other factors. On about the anniversary of the employee's appointment, assuming the employee has performed at least at the "fully successful" level in the job, the employee most likely (but not automatically) will be promoted to the next grade in the ladder. Most career ladders advance in two-grade intervals, from GS-5 to GS-7, from GS-7 to GS-9, and from GS-9 to GS-11. Once GS-11 is reached, promotions progress normally in one-grade intervals. Promotions to GS-14 and GS-15 are almost always the result of competition for a vacant position (U.S. Office of Personnel Management, 1991).

Another way to reward performance under GS is merit promotions across pay grades. Unlike the WGI, these competitive promotions are not "scheduled" according to tenure. They may be awarded to the employee at the discretion of the agency. Finally, the GS allows for performance-based noncash awards such as time off from duty, without loss of pay or vacation days, as an award in recognition of superior accomplishment. Table 6.2 summarizes how pay and promotions work in the GS system.

The GS pay system is based on complex, cumbersome, and outdated classification systems, but the day-to-day functioning is quite simple: Officials, in most cases, grant pay increases across the board automatically, and employees who serve a certain length of time at one grade level are in general promoted to the next grade level, regardless of their performance. In short, tenure counts much more than performance, especially if the employees are in grades 1–12; in grades 13–15, promotion is less automatic.

How Are Employees Evaluated?

Under the GS system, each agency may develop one or more appraisal systems. Some agencies use a 5-point rating (5 = outstanding, 4 = exceeds fully successful, 3 = fully successful, 2 = minimally successful, 1 = unacceptable); others use a 2-tiered pass–fail rating. To be awarded a career ladder promotion, an employee must typically earn a "pass" in the 2-tier system or, at least, a 3 ("fully successful") in the 5-point rating system. Because of its simplicity, the pass–fail rating is easier and more straightforward to implement than the 5-point rating system. The latter, however, allows for more distinction between adequate and high-quality workers.

Both systems are prone to leniency bias. The pass–fail rating may be prone to leniency bias at the lower end of the scale. That is, employees whose performance would have been rated below "fully successful" may be rated with a pass. But the leniency bias can be more pronounced in the 5-point system. It is subject to bias not just at the low end of the scale but at the high end as well, since giving a maximum rating of "outstanding" is easy for the supervisor, well received by employees, and has no real consequences in terms of budget (i.e., the highest rating does not necessarily result in additional pay).

Table 6.2
Pay and Promotions Under the GS Structure

Promotions	Basis	Competitiveness	Position
WGIs	Tenure	Noncompetitive	Within grade
QSIs	Performance	Noncompetitive[a]	Within grade
Cash/noncash awards	Performance	Noncompetitive	Within grade
Career ladder/targeted positions	Tenure[b]	Noncompetitive[c]	Across grades
Merit promotions	Performance	Competitive	Across grades
Establishment of new positions	—	Noncompetitive[a]	Across grades
Transfers	—	Competitive	Across grades

[a] Promotion is noncompetitive in terms of position, but may be competitive in terms of budget.

[b] Tenure is typical but not automatic.

[c] Promotions may become competitive in higher grades.

On the other hand, having numerous employees rated "outstanding" may not necessarily reflect leniency bias. It is possible to simply have an outstanding group of employees in an organization. This happened at the National Science Foundation (NSF) in 2005, when 66 percent of its senior executives were rated as "outstanding." Upon investigation, government officials found the rating justified (Halchin, 2005). However, when large groups of employees are rated at the top of the scale, the prestige of the system may be eroded.

Is Performance Evaluation Linked to Pay?

Pay and performance under the GS system are not very well linked. The WGIs reflect no link between pay and performance. All other things being equal, a mediocre employee will receive the WGI as fast as a better-performing colleague. As currently administered, the performance rating systems do not provide sufficient information to link pay with performance. It is likely that, because of the leniency bias, neither the pass–fail nor the 5-point system is capable of identifying poorly performing workers. Indeed, inflation of performance ratings for those who perform below acceptable levels of competence is a natural consequence of the way the GS is crafted by law. The onus is on supervisors to prove that an employee is an underperformer rather than on the employee to prove that he or she performs adequately, and employees are given every chance to prove their competence.

The common issues identified with the rare cases of poor performance are behavioral or conduct issues, substance abuse, or various illegal activities. Underperformers who do not exhibit any of these rather obvious problems may be rated as "fully successful." A study by the MSPB reported that many supervisors stated little negative cost for taking no action even when they are very aware of those common issues mentioned above (U.S. Office of Personnel Management, 1999). Neither the "fail" rating nor the "below 3" ratings are frequently used. As a result, low performance does not trigger financial losses such as losing a job or receiving a salary reduction. Likewise, supervisors do not receive any kind of penalty for being lenient in their evaluation. Moreover, leniency bias might be the rule in the case of politically appointed managers; more-pressing concerns prevent them from spending time disciplining poorly performing employees. To what extent leniency bias is exacerbated by this kind of behavior is a matter for further research.

With respect to high-quality employees, the pass–fail rating is simply too crude to provide any meaningful distinction between the mediocre and the outstanding. In theory, the 5-point rating system is better equipped to make this distinction, as it has more gradation. But, as discussed above, its potential to distinguish is undercut if there is leniency bias such that a large portion of employees are given a high rating, regardless of actual performance.

Even without leniency bias, a higher rating does not guarantee significantly higher pay as neither QSIs nor bonuses are automatic, even if an employee earns a rating of 5 ("outstanding"). Indeed, highly rated employees who are at the top step of their pay grade are not even eligible for a tenure-based raise, absent a promotion to a higher grade. And the onetime monetary rewards, which are given more frequently, are often only a few hundred dollars.

In summary, there is a little incentive under the GS structure to rise above mediocre performance because the additional effort may result in neither a distinction through the rating system nor through added compensation. The appraisal system, as used, does not produce ratings that are a strong proxy for performance.

Based on the lack of consequences for poor ratings and given the amount of time managers spend on appraisals, some other solutions have been proposed. For instance, Robert Behn of the John F. Kennedy School of Government at Harvard University argues that annual performance reviews undermine agencies' ability to fire truly bad employees. Behn claims that most agency managers have only two choices when trying to fire employees who do not pull their weight: Engage in a war with them or avoid the problem by giving them a passing grade. Behn suggests that the annual personnel appraisal wastes time and has had a pernicious effect by helping those who perform poorly hang on to their jobs. He would modify the system so that managers would have the chance to "leave the folder empty" as evidence of an employee's bad performance (Behn, 2006).

Measuring Substandard Performance in the Federal Government

In FY1998, the OPM conducted a survey of employees and supervisors in the federal government to examine the causes of poor performance, what has been done to address the problem, and what results have been achieved (U.S. Office of Personnel Management, 1999). The key findings were as follows:

- The best estimate of substandard performers in the federal workforce is 3.7 percent.
- There is no benchmark for comparison in either the public or the private sector. Some estimates for the U.S. private sector suggest a percentage of around 4 percent.
- Supervisors of poorly performing employees actively pursue solutions through both formal and informal means.
- Supervisors report having successfully rehabilitated a substantial number of poorly performing employees (around 40 percent).
- In the federal government, the legal protection for those who perform poorly is at least similar to the protection in the private sector and tends to be greater.
- Supervisors who had tackled poor performance successfully described the experience as intensely emotional and even "heroic."
- Although supervisors typically receive a general orientation on performance regulations and procedures during their initial supervisory training, they consider the assistance to be useless.

Is It Necessary to Modify the GS System?

Upon analyzing the civil service system and its effectiveness, Asch (2002) mentioned some basic characteristics of successful HR systems:

a. The HR system offers flexible personnel and compensation tools that efficiently promote the organization's mission.

b. Managers have discretion over how the personnel and compensation tools are used.

    c.   Managers have the incentive to use the personnel and compensation policies in a way that supports the organization's mission.

    d.   Resources are available to implement and monitor those policies.

    e.   Policies are transparent and appropriately linked to the organization's goals, and their implementation is subject to both internal and external oversight.

    f.   Policies are stable and limit the financial and career risks that workers face.

Although the GS structure has some of the features mentioned above (a, e, and f), the relevance of the other three (b, c, and d) depends on how agencies implement the system. According to Asch (2002), even though characteristics b, c, and d are not present in the current system, managers tend to not use the tools that the system has in order to allow some degree of flexibility.

Concerning the last two points, the system clearly defines conditions for promotion and salary growth, which results in a measure of transparency, but process also suffers from existing rigidities. These rigidities are particularly evident with respect to the entry and exit points of the ladder—hiring and firing. Light (2001), based on a survey of civil servants, found that civilian employees were dissatisfied with the hiring process and complained about the federal government's difficulties with regard to disciplining those who perform poorly.

In spite of all the rigidities in the GS, the scheme provides some tools for managers to use and achieve their goals (U.S. Office of Personnel Management, 2001). The "flexibility" tools—voluntary departures, recruitment, relocation, and retention—have not been widely used. Voluntary separations or buyout incentives can help managers in a downsizing process by allowing them to induce the separation of individuals in positions that are no longer needed (Asch, 2002). The number of buyouts agencies can offer is limited; for instance, the DoD offered 2,000 and 6,000 buyouts in 2002 and 2003, respectively, with a labor force of around 700,000 employees. Research has confirmed the effectiveness of using them in the military and attributes their limited usage elsewhere to the lack of funds and the bureaucratic process required to obtain approval for their use (Asch and Warner, 1999).

Recruitment, relocation, and retention ("3Rs") incentives have been also studied. Asch (2002) mentions that only 14 percent of all Executive Branch employees received 3Rs incentives in 1998, while only 1 percent of the new recruits had received bonuses. However, in recruiting the tendency is to increase the offering of bonuses: In FY2006, 47 agencies paid more than $140 million in bonuses to recruit, retain, and relocate employees compared with the $51 million that 35 agencies used in FY2005 (Barr, 2007c).

PART SEVEN

Some Departures from the GS

The DoD PFP Demonstration Projects

One of the early experiments on personnel decisions was the 1980 "China Lake" demonstration at the Naval Weapons Center in China Lake, California. The CSRA authorized a wide-ranging pilot program centered on the use of performance pay. The China Lake project was a pioneer among demonstration projects on PFP. It showed both an increase in performance and an overall increase in salary spending. Perceived to be a success, the PFP project gained permanent authorization at China Lake and additional demonstrations were authorized.

One of the most salient features of the demonstration projects is the option to use the "broadband" pay system, which is currently forbidden for agencies covered by 5 U.S.C. See the sidebar on page 26 (What Is Broadband Pay?) for the definition of broadbanding, a more flexible compensation scheme.

The period 1984–1993 saw the creation and termination of the PMRS. This system linked pay increases to performance for employees in the GS-13 to GS-15 pay grades. The program did not succeed and was terminated in 1993; its failure has been attributed to the widespread focus on process measurement as opposed to the outcomes that are at the core of PFP.

At the termination of the PRMS in 1993, five out of six PMRS employees were rated above "fully successful." The inflation of ratings drove the employees across the pay range at a faster pace. For example, it took only 9 years for a PMRS employee rated "outstanding" every year to move from the minimum to the maximum rate in the pay grade, compared with 18 years under the GS (assuming QSIs are not used). As a result, employees rated "outstanding" increased from 21 percent in 1985 to 41 percent in 1991 (U.S. Office of Personnel Management, 1996). The combination of the lack of budget control and the inflation of ratings impaired the credibility of the PMRS, which contributed to its termination in 1993.

The same problem has been encountered in the private sector. As a result, quotas and forced ranking systems are increasingly used. For instance, in the General Electric Company, only 20 percent of the staff may be rated at the highest level and at least 10 percent must be rated at the lowest level, using a three-level rating scale (OECD, 2005).

The perceived success of the China Lake project inspired reforms, leading Congress in 1994 to authorize the OPM to exert more effort to measure the benefits of PFP. In turn, the National Defense Authorization Act in 1995 empowered the DoD to expand the use of demonstration projects.

What Is Broadband Pay?

Broadband is a pay and classification approach that combines two or more grades into broad pay bands. The term "banding" is applied to the notion of grouping jobs horizontally (U.S. Office of Personnel Management, 1996).

Promotion raises do not occur as frequently in a broadband system as they do in narrow-range grade systems because there are fewer levels. But raises can be larger when they do occur.

With respect to general increases, each agency defines whether an automatic across-the-board increase will be granted to all employees and whether any general increase would impact the salary fund budget.

Broadband has been recommended for organizations that have specific characteristics: being in a stage of organizational reengineering, flattening structure and/or declining functional boundaries; having a strong performance-based culture and an effective performance management system; having top management who strongly support a performance culture; having effective communications channels within the organization; and having a well-designed, accurate budgeting and allocation system.

Theoretical considerations have also suggested the need for effective oversight within the organizations by external authorities. In the absence of monitoring, supervisors can engage in favoritism (Prendergast and Topel, 1996).

Pay banding has been widely used in the DoD demonstration projects. Yet, each demonstration project is different. They differ across the following factors:

- the use of competencies to evaluate employee performance
- how employee performance ratings translate into pay increases and awards
- how the costs of the PFP system are managed
- how information to employees about the results of performance appraisals and pay decisions is provided.

The specific features of three DoD demonstration projects are described below.

Air Force Research Lab (AFRL)

The AFRL uses the Contribution-Based Compensation System (CCS), the new model of an integrated approach to classification, compensation, and performance management. The CCS measures the contribution of employees to the mission of the organization based on six factors:

1. technical problem solving
2. communication/reporting
3. corporate resource management
4. technology transition/technology transfer
5. R&D business development
6. teamwork and leadership.

Weights assigned to these six factors vary according to the job category of the employee. Employees' pay decisions are determined by comparing their performance scores to their current salaries. The CCS score is plotted, compared with a Standard Pay Line. The pay decision depends on the "zone" in which the CCS score falls: If the score is within the Equitable Compensation zone, the minimum increase is equal to the general price index (GPI); if the score is in the Over-Compensated zone, the GPI is the maximum increase. And if the score is in the Under-Compensated zone, the increase includes both GPI and the incentives set by AFRL.

Navy Research Lab (NRL)

Similar to the AFRL, current salary is also considered in making performance-based decisions at the NRL. The objective is to make a better match between salary and contribution to the organization. Since current salary and contribution are jointly considered in determining pay increases and awards, two employees with comparable current salaries may have different pay increases because of different contributions to the organization. Similarly, employees with comparable contributions may have different pay increases or awards because of the difference in their current salaries.

The NRL's PFP system works by plotting contributions scores against employees' current salaries and a Standard Pay Line to determine if they are undercompensated, appropriately compensated, or overcompensated. Undercompensated employees receive the GPI and are eligible for pay increases and awards. Appropriately compensated employees may, likewise, receive the GPI, pay increase, and/or awards—but the pay increase should not move the employee outside the appropriate pay range. Overcompensated employees, meanwhile, may receive a reduced or no GPI and will not receive any increase or award.

Army Research Lab (ARL)

The ARL uses generic performance elements and evaluates overall performance on four levels: distinguished, commendable, successful, and unsatisfactory. Each performance element has an assigned weight that totals 100 points. The scores on each performance element are summed and averaged to determine the overall performance score, which has a maximum of 100. Only those with a score of "successful" or higher will receive GPIs, pay increases, and/or monetary rewards.

Lessons from PFP Demonstrations

Evaluations of the DoD compensation system suggest that the predemonstration system was "nonresponsive, bureaucratic, and failing to live up to its potential" (Asch, 2005, p. 313). But the formal evaluations of DoD demonstration projects were not highly favorable either. Asch concluded that "neither demonstration projects nor the waiver of Title 5 rules has led to markedly better outcomes" (Asch, 2005, p. 313).

In part, the absence of better outcomes may be attributable to some of the bureaucratic constraints imposed on the demonstrations. But the conceptual pitfalls of explicit PFP schemes identified in the literature (e.g., monitoring costs and inflated appraisals) were also difficult to overcome.

In 2004, the National Defense Authorization Act gave the DoD significant authority to redesign the rules, regulations, and processes that govern the way more than 700,000 defense civilian employees are hired, compensated, promoted, and disciplined. Under this new personnel system, called the National Security Personnel System (NSPS), a new salary system (replacing the GS scheme) is based on broad salary bands and PFP. The current plan is to convert all DoD employees into the new salary system by 2008. Proponents of NSPS argue that it could serve as a model for civil service reform for the entire federal government.

The DoD is not alone at the forefront of PFP in the federal government. The TSA has a Performance Accountability and Standards System (PASS). In 2005, the DHS adopted a new HR system, referred as MAXHR, with the objectives of achieving the highest level of individual performance and fostering accountability. Since the beginning of the program, MAXHR has encountered controversy and lawsuits, with unions expressing dissatisfaction with the new system.

The SES

SES includes most managerial, supervisory, and policy positions classified above GS-15. There are approximately 7,000 SES senior executives (Ketelaar, Manning, and Turkisch, 2007).

Internal and external candidates can be appointed to SES positions. Noncareer appointments—i.e., appointments on a competitive basis from outside the civil service—can only be made to general positions, cannot exceed 25 percent of an agency's SES position allocation, and governmentwide can be up to 10 percent of the SES positions (Halchin, 2005). After appointment to the SES, employees serve a one-year probationary period. If they do not perform satisfactorily during this period, they may be dismissed from the federal public service.

In 2004, a new performance system was introduced as part of an effort to better link individuals' contributions to service and program delivery with their pay. The previous pay system had six pay levels, and pay compression resulted in senior executives at the top three SES pay levels receiving essentially the same amount of base pay in a given year. With the introduction of the President's Management Agenda, the Bush administration has emphasized the need to connect PFP for senior executives to results, organizational excellence, and the administration's priorities and has criticized agency management systems that apparently fail to make meaningful distinctions among senior executives' job performances (Halchin, 2005).

In the new system, certain guidelines developed by the OPM are provided, but departments and agencies are free to determine the content and format for the performance agreements for senior civil servants. The new guidelines included, for example, the rule that 50 percent of the objectives are to be measurable, while the remaining 50 percent can be more qualitative. Through a yearly review and a certification process of agencies' performance appraisal systems, OPM retains quality control over the performance arrangement systems with the objective of ensuring consistency, transparency, and accountability in the whole appraisal process.

A performance agreement for a senior civil servant is linked to the objectives of the agency and should reflect the performance agreement of the line manager. Performance objectives are cascaded down the hierarchical line of responsibility. An individual senior civil servant will have program and corporate commitments. In addition to these commitments, a performance agreement can include competency requirements on which performance will be assessed.

If a civil servant has been promoted to a supervisory or managerial position and then fails to perform, he or she is returned to the previous position. Civil servants can be reassigned to other positions in case of poor performance. This can occur if there is an expectation of improved performance in the other position.

Ketelaar, Manning, and Turkisch (2007) point out that one of the main effects of the new performance arrangements is that agencies and departments are exercising more rigor in implementing PFP. In 2001, for instance, about 80 percent of senior civil servants received an evaluation at the level of "outstanding" that would warrant a performance bonus; in 2005, this percentage fell to 45 percent. This might be taken as an illustration that agencies and departments now give more thought to their evaluations.

In 2006, the SES was evaluated by the Senior Executives Association (SEA) and by the GAO. A survey of SES members by SEA found that, in spite of support for effective performance management, respondents have some complaints about how the system is working. De facto quotas (due the lack of funds) are affecting final performance ratings, and there remains a disconnect among ratings, pay adjustments, and bonuses. One of the pitfalls mentioned is the lack of adequate communication and a resultant lack of transparency. The majority report that motivation was not affected by the new system (Senior Executives Association and Avue Technologies Corporation, 2006).

The GAO found that, to successfully transform, an agency or department must reexamine its processes, organizational structures, and management approaches—including its workforce capacity and its organizational culture (U.S. Government Accountability Office, 2007). The GAO report also argues that communicating with stakeholders is crucial to success. High-performing organizations strengthen accountability by placing greater emphasis on collaboration, interaction, and teamwork across organizational boundaries, to achieve results that often transcend specific boundaries (U.S. Government Accountability Office, 2007).

FDIC and IRS

FDIC has an alternative HR system. It has worked through four iterations of its pay systems to finally find the one that is working and adapting to the agency needs. The agency's employee population increased from 4,000 to 23,000 but was later reduced to 5,000 in the late 1980s and early 1990s (Guerra, 2005).

FDIC tried various ways to change its performance management systems and combine full-time hires, contract employees, and returning retirees. FDIC organized new pay-for-performance bands—EM for executive management; CM for corporate management; and CG for corporate-grade, nonmanagerial positions—and also created a contribution-based compensation band, with five levels of merit raises and lump-sum payments for nonbargaining unit employees (Guerra, 2005). Since the introduction of its new personnel system, FDIC has faced 200 grievances and 40 arbitrations (Mendelsohn, 2007).

The IRS has had about 8,000 managers under a pay-for-performance system since September 2005. The IRS system has three components: a performance-based salary, the opportunity for a performance-based bonus, and a locality adjustment tied to average private-sector wages in the area where the person works (Barr, 2007d). Employees are rated on performance measures such as "fair and equitable treatment of taxpayers" and "customer satisfaction" (Walsh, 2006).

PART EIGHT

Proposals to Change the GS

Three bills in the 110th Congress attempt to address the GS system shortcomings: Senate bill 1045 (S. 1045) for federal employees in general and S. 1046 for senior-level and scientific and professional positions (Voinovich, 2007a, 2007b), and S. 967 (Akaka, 2007). These limited initiatives were partly a response to a more expansive White House proposal that that did not attract any sponsors in Congress (Working for America Act, 2005).

Table 8.1 outlines the similarities and differences between the status quo and the proposals. The White House proposal—the Working for America Act—seeks to identify and reward outstanding performance while also holding managers accountable for substandard performance. It also introduces pay banding and supports a more meaningful evaluation of employees by eliminating the pass–fail system.

S. 1045 identifies performance evaluation as the center of the implementation problem and addresses it by introducing training requirements for supervisors and by establishing a written evaluation report for each employee. Those who perform poorly are addressed by denying them the across-the-board wage increase (1.7 percent of base salary in 2007). S. 967

Table 8.1
Options for Change

Features	Status Quo	Proposed Legislation		
	GS	White House	S. 967	S. 1045
Training	NA	NA	Yes	Yes
Appraisal system	Allow the pass–fail rating system	Allow pass–fail only in the entry/developmental stage	NA	Eliminate the pass–fail rating; define the time and frequency of training to supervisors; prepare written performance appraisals annually
Pay banding	No	Yes (up to four categories by 2010)	NA	No
PFP	Continue using WGIs and QSIs, despite weak link between pay and performance	Require at minimum a rating of "fully successful"	NA	Explicitly link performance to the agency's strategic goals
Poor performance	NA	Deny pay increases for employees rated less than "fully successful"	NA	Deny pay increases for employees rated less than "fully successful"

recognizes the shortcomings associated with supervisor training and requires federal supervisors and managers to undergo training in setting performance goals, communicating them to employees, and motivating employees.

The Bush administration continues to promote performance pay in the federal government and has been moving toward implementing alternative personnel systems governmentwide. Starting in May 2005, federal agencies began completing small test runs for improved performance management systems. The beta sites are a chance to test the new personnel and payment system before extending it to the entire agency.

PART NINE

Burgeoning Opposition to PFP

PFP has attracted opposition not only from labor unions but also from key members of Congress. The resistance has been manifested in lawsuits and legislative efforts to deny funding for PFP implementation or rescind the authority to implement PFP. The dispute over PFP is part of a larger dispute about the collective bargaining rights of civil servants.

The TSA

In creating the TSA after the September 11, 2001, terrorist attacks, Congress provided the Bush administration with broad leeway to set the terms and conditions of employment for passenger and baggage screeners. Citing national security considerations and the need for different work rules at the nation's 400 airports, the TSA decided to not permit collective bargaining for screeners. Instead, the TSA became one of the few large federal agencies to operate with a performance-based pay system.

In December 2006, the TSA unveiled the PASS compensation packages for 2007. Under the system, TSA screeners receive an annual pay raise and locality adjustment, similar to those provided other federal employees, but they may receive an additional raise and bonus based on their job performance ratings. In 2007, for example, a screener rated at the highest level received a 1.7 percent raise, an average locality adjustment of 0.5 percent, a 5 percent performance raise, and a $3,000 lump-sum bonus.

The National Treasury Employees Union has complained that only a small percentage of the transportation security officers received job ratings that permitted them to qualify for a merit-based salary increase. The TSA reports that about $37 million was paid in performance-based pay and bonuses in the second half of 2006, after the system's start. An additional $58 million was paid to employees in February 2007.

Unions have filed lawsuits to stop the new systems at the TSA and DHS, saying they jeopardize the bargaining rights of workers. The litigation has slowed the implementation of PFP systems, and it may take years to fully resolve the litigation.

One of the salient rulings was in a case brought by a union and John Gavello, who was fired from the TSA in 2004. The government countered that screeners were excluded from civil service job protections when the TSA was created in 2001. The U.S. District Court for the Northern District of California in 2004 agreed with the government, but that decision was reversed by the U.S. Court of Appeals for the 9th Circuit (*AFGE Local 1 v. Stone*, 2007). The case was sent back to the district court for reconsideration. Gavello's case is part of a larger effort by organized labor to win bargaining rights and union protections for security officers at the TSA.

In addition to their litigation strategy, unions are urging Congress to repeal TSA authority to avoid collective bargaining and implement PFP. In a mostly party-line vote in March 2007, Senate Democrats upheld a move to restore the collective bargaining rights of TSA employees (Yoest, 2007). Earlier in 2007, the House passed a bill that revived collective bargaining rights (Yoest and Starks, 2007). President Bush pledged a veto. The House vote margin of 299–128 was greater than the two-thirds majority needed to override a presidential veto, but the Senate vote of 51–46 fell short of the 66 needed to override.

Meanwhile, opposition to funding PFP has grown. For example, in the 2008 TSA appropriations bill, the Senate provided only $5 million out of the $15 million sought for the new system (Barr, 2007b). The House approved no funding, saying that money should not be spent until "all pending litigation is resolved."

In September 2007, the TSA announced that it is planning to alter its PFP system in 2008. One modification will change the number of rating levels from four to five, giving all employees classified in the top three levels at least a small salary increase and bonus. Formerly, only employees given the two top ratings were eligible for pay increases. In 2006, only 2 percent of employees received the highest rating of "role model," and only 20 percent got the next-highest mark of "exceeds standards." In the most recent ratings, 96 percent of the screeners were rated as achieving or exceeding TSA standards, making them eligible for cash bonuses (Barr, 2007b).

Opposition to the DoD's PFP Scheme

In early September 2007, the U.S. House of Representatives approved an amendment to the FY2008 Defense appropriations bill, which prohibits the DoD from using any funds to implement NSPS, including the use of PFP. President Bush issued a veto threat. The Senate voted 92–3 in favor of the FY2008 Defense authorization bill (Ballenstedt, 2007). It repeals the Pentagon's authority to implement the labor relations portions of its NSPS and permits the Pentagon to continue developing a PFP system as long as such a system would be consistent with federal labor relations law, but excludes blue-collar workers from NSPS.

Union litigation against implementation of the NSPS is also ongoing. In 2006, a U.S. District Court judge ruled that NSPS violates collective bargaining rights. In May 2007, an appeals court overturned that decision by a 2-to-1 vote, giving the DoD the go-ahead to implement the system. In September 2007, the U.S. Court of Appeals for the District of Columbia denied a motion by a coalition of unions for a full court review (*AFGE v. Gates*, 2007).

The DoD and DHS appropriation bills have not been signed by President Bush. In the last week of September 2007, Congress approved a continuing resolution to fund the federal government through December 14, 2007, to allow time to resolve differences of opinion.

In our view, Congress should not prohibit or scale back PFP until the current experience is evaluated with care. Regardless of what Congress and the current administration decide to do, the next administration should move to establish pay systems that penalize poor performance and reward outstanding performance, facilitate dialogue with employees and unions, and extend and evaluate pilot tests of new HR systems. A return to the GS structure is a step backward.

References

AFGE (American Federation of Government Employees) Local 1 v. Stone, No. 05-15206, United States Court of Appeals for the Ninth Circuit, September 5, 2007.

AFGE v. Gates, No. 06-5113, United States Court of Appeals for the District of Columbia Circuit, September 5, 2007.

Akaka, Daniel, Federal Supervisor Training Act of 2007, Senate bill 967, Washington, D.C., 2007.

Asch, Beth J., *Ensuring Successful Personnel Management in the Department of Homeland Security*, Santa Monica, Calif.: RAND Corporation, IP-235-NSRD, 2002. As of November 30, 2007: http://www.rand.org/pubs/issue_papers/IP235/

———, "The Economic Complexities of Incentive Reforms," in Robert Klitgaard and Paul C. Light, eds., *High-Performance Government: Structure, Leadership, Incentives*, Santa Monica, Calif.: RAND Corporation, MG-256-PRGS, 2005, pp. 309–342. As of November 30, 2007: http://www.rand.org/pubs/monographs/MG256/

Asch, Beth J., and John T. Warner, *Separation and Retirement Incentives in the Federal Civil Service: A Comparison of the Federal Employees Retirement System and the Civil Service Retirement System*, Santa Monica, Calif.: RAND Corporation, MR-986-OSD, 1999. As of November 30, 2007: http://www.rand.org/pubs/monograph_reports/MR986/

Ballenstedt, Brittany R., "Senate Moves to Restrict Defense Personnel Overhaul," *Government Executive.com*, October 2, 2007. As of November 30, 2007: http://www.govexec.com/story_page.cfm?articleid=38194&sid=59

Barr, Stephen, "Bonuses Blossom in Senior Executives' Compensation," *The Washington Post*, June 26, 2007a, p. D04.

———, "A Closer Inspection of Airport Screeners' Pay," *The Washington Post*, July 31, 2007b, p. D04.

———, "More Bonuses Used for Recruiting and Retention," *The Washington Post*, September 12, 2007c, p. D04.

———, "IRS Reviews Performance-Based Pay for Managers," *The Washington Post*, September 25, 2007d, p. D04.

Behn, Robert D., "End Annual Personnel Appraisals," *Bob Behn's Public Management Report*, Vol. 3, No. 5, January 2006. As of November 30, 2007: http://www.ksg.harvard.edu/thebehnreport/January2006.pdf

Benedict, Michael E., and Edward L. Levine, "Delay and Distortion: Tacit Influences on Performance Appraisal Effectiveness," *Journal of Applied Psychology*, Vol. 73, No. 3, August 1988, pp. 507–514.

Bretz, Robert D., Jr., George T. Milkovich and Walter Read, "The Current State of Performance Appraisal Research and Practice: Concerns, Directions, and Implications," Center for Advanced Human Resource Studies (CAHRS), CAHRS Working Paper No. 92-15, Ithaca, N.Y.: Cornell University, 1992. As of November 30, 2007: http://digitalcommons.ilr.cornell.edu/cahrswp/298

Burgess, Simon, and Marisa Ratto, "The Role of Incentives in the Public Sector: Issues and Evidence," *Oxford Review of Economic Policy*, Vol. 19, No. 2, Summer 2003, pp. 285–300.

Damp, Dennis V., *The Book of U.S. Government Jobs: Where They Are, What's Available, and How to Get One*, 8th ed., Washington, D.C.: Bookhaven Press LLC, 2002.

Gootman, Elissa, "Bloomberg Unveils Performance Pay for Teachers," *The New York Times*, October 17, 2007.

Guerra, John L., "To Cope with Change, FDIC Becomes Lab for Alternative Pay Systems," *Government Leader*, October 18, 2005. As of November 30, 2007:
http://www.governmentleader.com/issues/news/69-1.html

Halchin, L. Elaine, "Senior Executive Service (SES) Pay System," Congressional Research Service Report RL33128, Washington, D.C.: Congressional Research Service, October 25, 2005. As of November 30, 2007:
http://digital.library.unt.edu/govdocs/crs/permalink/meta-crs-7914:1

Ingraham, Patricia W., "Pay for Performance in the States," *The American Review of Public Administration*, Vol. 23, No. 3, September 1993, pp. 189–200.

Kellough, J. Edward, and Lloyd G. Nigro, "Pay for Performance in Georgia State Government: Employee Perspectives on GeorgiaGain After 5 Years," *Review of Public Personnel Administration*, Vol. 22, No. 2, June 2002, pp. 146–166.

Kellough, J. Edward, and Sally Coleman Selden, "Pay-for-Performance Systems in State Government: Perceptions of State Agency Personnel Managers," *Review of Public Personnel Administration*, Vol. 17, No. 1, January 1997, pp. 5–21.

Ketelaar, Anne, Nick Manning, and Edouard Turkisch, "Performance-Based Arrangements for Senior Civil Servants: OECD and Other Countries' Experiences," *OECD Working Papers on Public Governance*, 2007/5, Paris: OECD Publishing, 2007. As of November 30, 2007:
http://www.oecd.org/dataoecd/11/40/38990099.pdf

Lazear, Edward P., *Personnel Economics*, Cambridge, Mass.: MIT Press, 1995.

———, "Performance Pay and Productivity," NBER Working Paper Series No. 5672, Cambridge, Mass.: National Bureau of Economic Research, 1996. As of November 30, 2007:
http://www.nber.org/papers/w5672

———, "Performance Pay and Productivity," *The American Economic Review*, Vol. 90, No. 5, December 2000, pp. 1346–1361.

Light, Paul C., "To Restore and Renew: Now Is the Time to Rebuild the Federal Public Service," Washington, D.C.: The Brookings Institution, November 2001. As of November 30, 2007:
http://www.brookings.edu/views/articles/light/200111ge.htm

Marsden, David, "The Role of Performance-Related Pay in Renegotiating the 'Effort Bargain': The Case of the British Public Service," *Industrial & Labor Relations Review*, Vol. 57, No. 3, April 2004, pp. 350–370.

Marsden, David, and Stephen French, "What a Performance: Performance Related Pay in the Public Services," Special Report, London: Centre for Economic Performance, London School of Economics, 1998.

Melkers, Julia, and Katherine Willoughby, "Evolving Performance Measurement in Local Governments," presented at the 2002 meeting of the Association for Budgeting and Financial Management, Kansas City, Mo., 2002. As of November 30, 2007:
http://unpan1.un.org/intradoc/groups/public/documents/ASPA/UNPAN005914.pdf

Mendelsohn, Randi, "Pay for Performance: Effectively Managing and Rewarding Employees at the Federal Deposit Insurance Corporation," presentation, 2007. As of November 30, 2007:
http://www.ipma-hr.org/ppt/Track3_3_FDIC.ppt#323,25,Slide 25

Milkovich, George T., and Alexandra K. Wigdor, eds., *Pay for Performance: Evaluating Performance Appraisal and Merit Pay*, Commission on Behavioral and Social Sciences and Education (CBASSE), Washington, D.C.: The National Academies Press, 1991.

Mount, M. K., and D. E. Thompson, "Cognitive Categorization and Quality of Performance Ratings," *Journal of Applied Psychology*, Vol. 72, No. 2, May 1987, pp. 240–246.

OECD, *Public Service Pay Determination and Pay Systems in OECD Countries*, PUMA Occasional Paper No. 2, Paris, Organisation for Economic Co-operation and Development, 1994.

———, *Performance-Related Pay Policies for Government Employees*, Paris: OECD Publishing, June 2005.

Podgursky, Michael J., and Matthew G. Springer, "Teacher Performance Pay: A Review," *Journal of Policy Analysis and Management*, Vol. 26, No. 4, Autumn 2007, pp. 909–950.

Porter, Lyman W., and Edward E. Lawler, *Managerial Attitudes and Performance*, Homewood, Ill.: Dorsey Press, 1968.

Prendergast, Canice, "The Provision of Incentives in Firms," *Journal of Economic Literature*, Vol. 37, No. 1, March 1999, pp. 7–63.

Prendergast, Canice, and Robert H. Topel, "Favoritism in Organizations," *Journal of Political Economy*, Vol. 104, No. 5, October 1996, pp. 958–978.

Risher, Howard, *Pay for Performance: A Guide for Federal Managers*, Human Capital Management Series, IBM Center for The Business of Government, November 2004. As of November 30, 2007: http://www.businessofgovernment.org/pdfs/RisherReport.pdf

Senior Executives Association and Avue Technologies Corporation, *Survey of the Senior Executive Service Pay and Performance Management System: Lost in Translation*, 2006. As of November 30, 2007: http://seniorexecs.org/fileadmin/user_upload/SEA_Mainstays/SEA_Avue_Pay_For_Performance_Suvery_Results_Report.pdf

United States Code, Title 5, Government Organization and Employees: Part II (Civil Service Functions and Responsibilities) and Part III (Employees). As of November 30, 2007: http://www.access.gpo.gov/uscode/title5/title5.html

U.S. General Accounting Office, *Pay for Performance: State and International Public Sector Pay-for-Performance Systems*, GAO/GGD-91-1, Washington, D.C., October 1990.

———, *Implementing Pay for Performance at Selected Personnel Demonstration Projects*, Report to Congressional Requesters, GAO-04-83, Washington, D.C., January 2004. As of November 30, 2007: http://www.gao.gov/new.items/d0483.pdf

U.S. Government Accountability Office, *Key Lessons Learned to Date for Strengthening Capacity to Lead and Implement Human Capital Reforms*, Report to Congressional Requesters, GAO-07-90, Washington, D.C., January 2007. As of November 30, 2007: www.gao.gov/cgi-bin/getrpt?GAO-07-90

U.S. Office of Personnel Management, *The Classifier's Handbook*, TS-107, Washington, D.C., August 1991. As of November 30, 2007: http://www.opm.gov/fedclass/clashnbk.pdf

———, *Alternative Pay Progression Strategies: Broadbanding Applications*, Performance Management Series, PMD-05, Washington, D.C., April 1996. As of November 30, 2007: http://www.opm.gov/perform/articles/pdf2.asp

———, *Poor Performers in Government: A Quest for the True Story*, Washington, D.C., January 1999. As of November 30, 2007: http://www.opm.gov/studies/perform.pdf

———, Office of Merit Systems Effectiveness, Center for HR Innovation, *Human Resources Flexibilities and Authorities in the Federal Government*, Washington, D.C., July 2001 (updated April 2002). As of November 30, 2007: http://www.opm.gov/omsoe/hr-flex/

———, Strategic Compensation Policy Center, *Evolution of Federal White-Collar Pay*, Washington, D.C., 2007. As of November 30, 2007: http://www.opm.gov/strategiccomp/HTML/HISTORY1.asp

Voinovich, George, Federal Workforce Performance Appraisal and Management Improvement Act of 2007, Senate bill 1045, Washington, D.C., 2007a.

———, Senior Professional Performance Act of 2007, Senate bill 1046, Washington, D.C., 2007b.

Vroom, Victor H., *Work and Motivation*, New York: Wiley, 1964.

Walsh, Trudy, "Performance Anxiety," *Government Leader*, Vol. 1, No. 5, January/February 2006. As of November 30, 2007:
http://www.governmentleader.com/issues/1_5/features/107-1.html

Working for America Act, draft, 2005. As of November 30, 2007:
http://www.whitehouse.gov/results/agenda/facts-about-draft-bill.pdf

Yoest, Patrick, "9/11 Bill Takes Shape for Senate Vote," *CQ Weekly*, March 12, 2007, pp. 750–751.

Yoest, Patrick, and Tim Starks, "First to Pass Sept. 11 Provisions," *CQ Weekly*, January 15, 2007, pp. 180–181.

Related Readings

Ballenstedt, Brittany R., "TSA to Modify Screener Pay System," *Government Executive.com*, September 27, 2007. As of November 30, 2007:
http://www.govexec.com/story_page.cfm?articleid=38147

Barr, Stephen, "Is the Annual Performance Review the Goof-Off's Best Friend?" *The Washington Post*, January 10, 2006, p. B02.

————, "Defense Switching More Workers to NSPS," *The Washington Post*, July 13, 2006, p. D04.

————, "TSA Screeners May Get Union Rights," *The Washington Post*, January 9, 2007, p. D04.

————, "Senate Panel to Senior Feds: Improve Your People Skills," *The Washington Post*, June 15, 2007, p. D04.

————, "New Personnel System Hits Another Snag," *The Washington Post*, August 7, 2007, p. D04.

————, "Bill Pushes Diversity Among Senior Executives," *The Washington Post*, October 5, 2007, p. D04.

Danker, Tony, Thomas Dohrmann, Nancy Killefer, and Lenny Mendonca, "How Can American Government Meet Its Productivity Challenge?" *McKinsey in the News*, October 2006. As of November 30, 2007:
http://www.mckinsey.com/aboutus/mckinseynews/americangovt_prodchallenge.asp

Dixit, Avinashi, "Incentives and Organizations in the Public Sector: An Interpretative Review," *Journal of Human Resources*, Vol. 37, No. 4, Fall 2002, pp. 696–727.

Locke, Edwin A., and Gary P. Latham, *A Theory of Goal Setting and Task Performance*, Englewood Cliffs, N.J.: Prentice-Hall, 1990.

Robinson, Brian, "FDIC Succeeds at New Pay Plan: A Small Agency Has Lessons for Others Looking at Pay-for-Performance Plans," *FCW.com Story*, June 13, 2005. As of November 30, 2007:
http://www.fcw.com/print/11_24/news/89136-1.html

Rosenberg, Alyssa, "Arbitrator Rules for Union in Dispute with IRS," *Government Executive.com*, September 26, 2007. As of November 30, 2007:
http://www.govexec.com/story_page.cfm?articleid=38135&sid=59

Rutzick, Karen, "Demonstration Projects Find Success in Personnel Reform," *Government Executive.com*, September 27, 2005. As of November 30, 2007:
http://www.govexec.com/dailyfed/0905/092705r1.htm

————, "Agencies Test New Performance Management Systems," *Government Executive.com*, June 5, 2006. As of November 30, 2007:
http://www.govexec.com/dailyfed/0606/060506r1.htm

————, "Paybanding Evolution," *Government Executive.com*, April 19, 2007. As of November 30, 2007:
http://www.governmentexecutive.com/story_page.cfm?articleid=36660&ref=rellink

Tarallo, Mark, "Agreed: Managers Need More Prep for Performance Appraisals," *Government Leader*, Vol. 1, No. 9, September/October 2006. As of November 30, 2007:
http://www.governmentleader.com/issues/1_9/upshot/201-1.html

U.S. General Accounting Office, *Federal Downsizing: Effective Buyout Practices and Their Use in FY 1997*, GAO/GGD-97-124, Washington, D.C., June 1997. As of November 30, 2007:
http://www.gao.gov/archive/1997/gg97124.pdf

U.S. Government Accountability Office, *DoD's National Security Personnel System Faces Implementation Challenges*, Report to Congressional Committees, GAO-05-730, Washington, D.C., July 2005. As of November 30, 2007:
http://www.gao.gov/new.items/d05730.pdf

U.S. Office of Personnel Management, *A Fresh Start for Federal Pay: The Case for Modernization*, Washington, D.C., April 2002. As of November 30, 2007:
http://www.opm.gov/strategiccomp/whtpaper.pdf